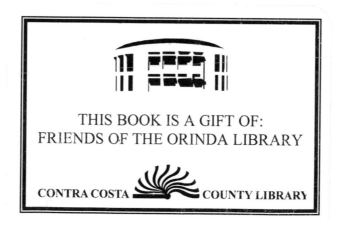

The Primary Source Library of Famous Explorers™

Sir Francis Drake

A Primary Source Biography

Lynn Hoogenboom

WITHDRAWN

The Rosen Publishing Group's

PowerKids Press™
PRIMARY SOURCE

New York

For Charlotte

Published in 2006 by The Rosen Publishing Group, Inc.
29 East 21st Street, New York, NY 10010

First Edition

Editor: Daryl Heller
Book Design: Albert B. Hanner
Photo Researcher: Fernanda Rocha

Photo Credits: Cover © Getty Images; p. 5 (top) Victoria & Albert Museum, London, UK/Bridgeman Art Library; p. 5 (bottom) map by
Albert Hanner; p. 6 (left) The National Archives of the United Kingdom (PRO), SP 12/44, f. 16; pp. 6 (right), 9 (top) Private
Collection/Bridgeman Art Library; p. 9 (bottom) Mary Evans/Douglas McCarthy; p. 10 (left) akg-images; p. 10 (right) The Art
Archive/Maritiem Museum Prins Hendrik Rotterdam/Dagli Orti; p. 13 (top) The Art Archive/British Library/British Library; p. 13 (bottom)
The Art Archive/Arquivo Nacional da Torre do Tombo Lisbon/Dagli Orti; p. 14 (top) Library of Congress Geography and Map
Division; p. 14 (bottom) Mary Evans Picture Library; p. 17 (top) © Baldwin H. Ward & Kathryn C. Ward/Corbis; p. 17 (bottom) The
Pierpont Morgan Library/Art Resource, NY, MA 3900, f. 4v; p. 18 (top) © British Library/HIP/Art Resource, NY; p. 18 (bottom) The
Art Archive/Plymouth Art Gallery/Eileen Tweedy; p. 21 © Public Record Office/Topham-HIP/The Image Works.

Library of Congress Cataloging-in-Publication Data

Hoogenboom, Lynn.
 Sir Francis Drake : a primary source biography / Lynn Hoogenboom.— 1st ed.
     p. cm. — (The primary source library of famous explorers)
 Includes index.
 ISBN 1-4042-3035-1 (lib. bdg.)
 1. Drake, Francis, Sir, 1540?–1596—Juvenile literature. 2. Great Britain—History, Naval—Tudors, 1485–1603—Juvenile literature.
3. Great Britain—History—Elizabeth, 1558–1603—Biography—Juvenile literature. 4. America—Discovery and exploration—
English—Juvenile literature. 5. Explorers—Great Britain—Biography—Juvenile literature. 6. Admirals—Great Britain—Biography—
Juvenile literature. I. Title. II. Series: Hoogenboom, Lynn. Primary source library of famous explorers.
 DA86.22.D7H627 2006
 942.05'5'092—dc22

                          2004025432

Manufactured in the United States of America

Contents

Childhood

Francis Drake was born around 1540 in Tavistock, England. Birth records no longer exist, so historians cannot be sure of the exact date. His father was Edmund Drake, and his mother's name may have been Anna. Francis's father was a shearman, or someone who used scissors to smooth out the surface of cloth. This skill was needed because handmade cloth was often bumpy. Edmund Drake was also a **Protestant** priest, or a religious official, for the Church of England.

Francis probably had many brothers and sisters, but historians do not know the number. In those days parents often sent their children to live with richer relatives. When Drake was a boy, he was sent to live with his cousin Sir John Hawkins.

Hawkins lived in Plymouth, which was on the southern coast of England. Hawkins was a shipper. A shipper moves goods from one place to another. While Drake was living with the Hawkins family, he traveled to Holland, France, and Spain. He also learned how to handle a ship.

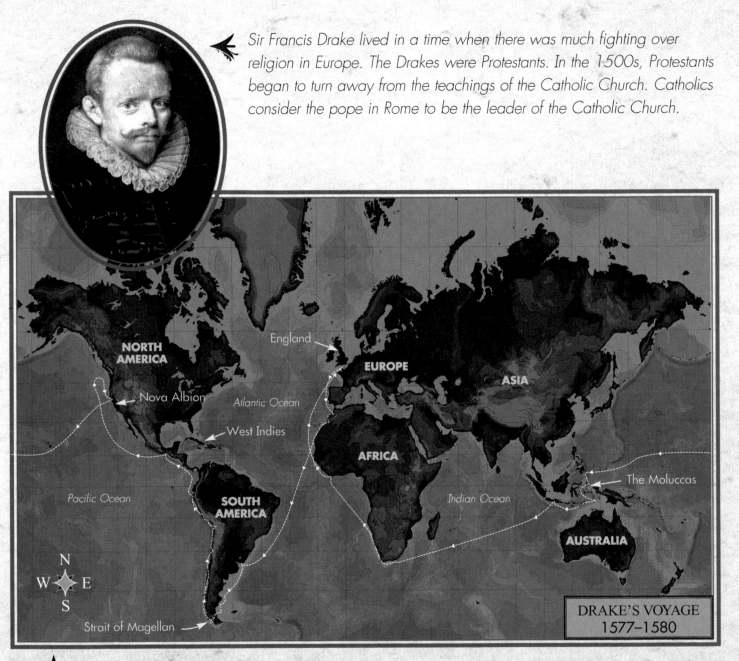

Sir Francis Drake lived in a time when there was much fighting over religion in Europe. The Drakes were Protestants. In the 1500s, Protestants began to turn away from the teachings of the Catholic Church. Catholics consider the pope in Rome to be the leader of the Catholic Church.

DRAKE'S VOYAGE
1577–1580

This map shows the route Sir Francis Drake took on his 1577–1580 voyage around the world. Drake left Plymouth, England, in 1577. Among the many places he landed or sailed to after crossing the Atlantic Ocean were the Strait of Magellan and Nova Albion. On his return to England, Drake stopped at the Moluccas, a group of islands that is modern-day Indonesia. Drake then sailed around the southern tip of Africa before heading north to England.

Sir John Hawkins benefited when Elizabeth became queen of England because Elizabeth allowed Hawkins to trade in Africa. During this period in history most Europeans thought there was nothing wrong with enslaving anyone who was not a Christian, or a person who followed the beliefs of Jesus Christ. Hundreds of years would pass before people recognized the cruelty of the slave trade.

On September 16, 1567, Sir John Hawkins wrote this letter to Queen Elizabeth seeking her permission to go to the African coast to capture Africans.

From John Hawkins's Letter to Queen Elizabeth

"The voyadge I pretend ys to lade Negoes in Genoya and sell them in the west Indyes in troke of golde perrles and Esmeraldes whereof I dowte not but to bring home in great abondance."

This sentence means that Hawkins planned to sell Africans into slavery in the West Indies. He would use the money to bring the queen a great sum of gold, pearls, and emeralds.

6

The Early Voyages

During the 1500s, Portugal and Spain controlled the major **trade routes** in the Atlantic Ocean. Portugal blocked other countries from trading with Africa and Brazil. Spain barred other countries from trading with America. Shippers from other countries sometimes traded along those routes anyway. In 1562, Francis Drake sailed with John Hawkins on the first slave-trading **voyage** in English history. The ships stopped first in Africa to capture Africans. Then they traveled to the West Indies, the islands in the Caribbean Sea between North America and South America. Here the Africans were sold to the Spanish as slaves. Hawkins charged less for slaves than Spanish traders did, so the Spanish traded with him even though it was forbidden.

Drake commanded one of the smaller ships on a slave-trading **expedition** that lasted from 1567 to 1569. On that trip the Spanish attacked the English ships in the West Indies. One of the English ships sank and several were captured. Drake and Hawkins were able to escape.

In Search of Spanish Treasure

On July 4, 1569, Francis Drake married a woman named Mary Newman in England. In 1570, he led two ships to the West Indies. This time he sailed as a **pirate**. The Spanish were shipping huge amounts of gold and silver from America to Spain. Drake was looking for places where Spanish **treasure** could be stolen.

Drake captured several Spanish ships in 1571. Some of them had **valuable cargoes**, and the voyage was a financial success. Drake's name began to cause fear in the West Indies. In 1572, Drake sailed to Central America to look for riches. He and a French partner, Guillaume Le Testu, went on land. They attacked a Spanish **mule train** carrying gold and silver. The partners were aided by cimarrones, who were escaped African slaves living in the hills of Central America. Le Testu was wounded in the attack and died. Drake, however, carried away a large sum of gold and silver worth about 40,000 pounds. He returned to England a wealthy man.

FRANCISCVS DRAECK · NOBILISSIMVS EQVES ANGLIAE · IS EST QVI TOTO T ORBE CRCMDVGO

After Drake and his men successfully attacked a Spanish mule train near a Spanish settlement, they brought the stolen treasure back to their ship and sailed away.

The cimarrones, or escaped African slaves, served as spies for Francis Drake. They told him where and when he should attack to gain the Spaniards' gold and silver.

Sailors who unlawfully attack ships and steal their cargoes are called pirates. During wars or when countries are close to fighting, a government will sometimes give privately owned ships permission to attack the ships that sail for the enemy country. These ships and their sailors are called privateers.

9

This compass was made in 1568. Sailors at sea depended on compasses for direction. The metal needle on a compass points north. Over time the English made many improvements to the compass.

This painted wooden figurehead from the 1600s was used to decorate a pirate's ship. A figurehead was usually placed on the front of a ship. Francis Drake and his cousin John Hawkins were both pirates.

Across the Atlantic

By the time Francis Drake returned to England, relations with Spain had improved. This meant that Drake could no longer openly attack Spanish ships and towns in the West Indies. Therefore, in 1575, Drake went to Ireland to fight alongside the Earl of Essex. England was in control of Ireland. Essex was trying to remove Irish landowners, so their lands could be given to English people.

After helping Essex, Drake planned a voyage with Thomas Doughty. He was a soldier Drake had met in Ireland. The plans were kept secret. The men intended to attack Spanish ships and towns on the Pacific coast of South America. Captain Drake and Doughty set out with five ships on December 13, 1577. As they crossed the Atlantic, Drake began to feel that Doughty was not obeying him. Doughty believed they were partners, or equals, and spoke against Drake. As the ships neared the southern tip of South America, Drake put Doughty on trial for **mutiny**. Doughty was found guilty, and Drake had him killed.

The Strait of Magellan

On August 21, 1578, Francis Drake's ships entered the **Strait** of Magellan hoping to reach the Pacific Ocean. Drake had reduced his **fleet** to three ships before attempting to sail the unsafe strait. The strait is a narrow waterway at South America's southern tip. In addition to being narrow, the strait is also rocky with strong winds and powerful currents. Ferdinand Magellan, the first man to sail around the world, had discovered the strait in 1520.

In Drake's time people thought there was a large continent south of the strait. They thought that this waterway was the only way to get from the Atlantic Ocean to the Pacific Ocean. Magellan had taken 37 days to get through the strait. **Amazingly**, Drake took only 16 days. However, once the ships safely passed through the strait, a horrible storm hit. Drake lost two ships. One of them sank. The other ship could not find Drake and returned to England.

Francis Fletcher was a priest who was on Francis Drake's voyage of 1577. Fletcher took notes on the Native Americans, animals, and plants he saw on this trip. Included were notes on a seal that he saw in the Bay of Montevideo. The drawing was probably done by another person who sailed on the same voyage.

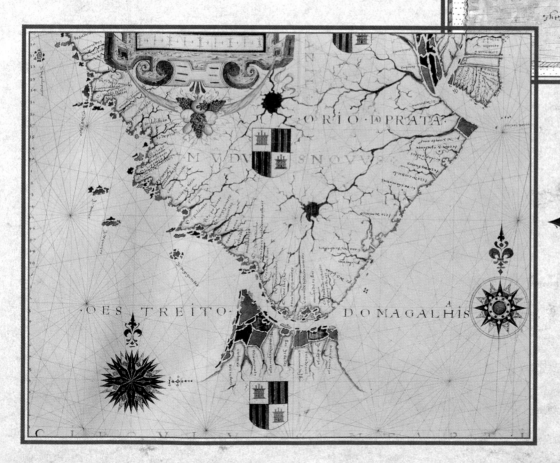

This map appeared in a 1571 atlas, or a collection of maps. The Strait of Magellan, a waterway that cuts across the tip of South America, is shown near the bottom of this map.

This map of the world was created around 1595 to record Drake's voyage around the world. The Dutch mapmaker added drawings to guide readers as they followed Drake's route on paper. In the upper left corner of the map is a smaller map of Nova Albion in modern-day California.

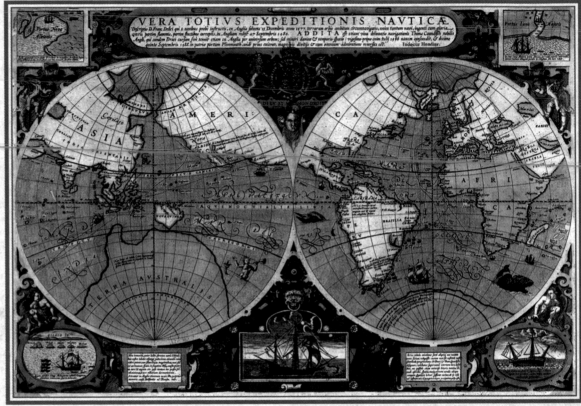

The Golden Hind, *the ship that took Francis Drake and his crew around the world, was first called the Pelican. Historians are not sure when it came to be called the Golden Hind. It was the largest ship in Drake's fleet. Drake used some of his own money to build the ship in England around 1574. One of the men who sailed on the Golden Hind said the ship was fast, well made, and armed with a number of guns.*

To the Pacific and Beyond

After reaching the Pacific, Francis Drake traveled north up the western coast of South America. Drake and his men attacked Spanish ships in **ports** along the way. Drake captured a huge amount of gold and silver. He could not return to England the way he came because the Spaniards would try to catch him.

To return Drake would need to sail around the world. Drake continued north past Mexico. He stopped to fix his ship at a place he named Nova Albion, or New England. Many historians think this area was just north of San Francisco, California.

Drake left America in July 1579 and sailed west across the Pacific. Drake stopped in the Moluccas, or modern-day Indonesia, where he bought spices. In the Indian Ocean Drake's ship, the *Golden Hind,* got stuck on a **reef**. Luckily a storm blew the ship off the rocks. Drake then sailed around Africa and back to England.

Fame and Fortune

Francis Drake arrived home in Plymouth, England, in September 1580. The huge fortune he had taken from the Spanish and his successful trip around the world made him a national hero. Drake soon purchased a large house and property near Plymouth that was called Buckland Abbey.

On April 1, 1581, Queen Elizabeth **knighted** him, and he became Sir Francis Drake. After his return Drake also served in **Parliament** and as the mayor of Plymouth.

There was some unpleasantness, though. Thomas Doughty's brother John charged Drake with murdering Doughty. Queen Elizabeth, however, was quite pleased with the gold Drake had taken from the Spanish. She made sure the case against Drake went nowhere.

In 1583, Drake's wife Mary died. Drake married Elizabeth Sydenham in 1585. She was a wealthy young woman from a respected family.

Queen Elizabeth knighted Sir Francis Drake on board the Golden Hind in Deptford, England, on April 1, 1581. So many people came to witness the event that the board used to climb onto the ship broke and many guests fell into the water. It was common for people from wealthy families to be knighted. However, it was unusual that someone who grew up in a poor family, as Francis Drake had, would be given such an honor.

PETVN

When Drake returned to England from a 1585 voyage to the New World, he brought back a plant called tobacco that was grown by Native Americans.

When Elizabeth became queen of England in 1558, there was fighting across the country between Catholics and Protestants. As queen, Elizabeth made the Church of England Protestant but kept many Catholic practices in the church. The English government also owed a great deal of money. Elizabeth made sure the government stopped wasting money. She ruled for 45 years.

Sir Francis Drake helped lead the English fleet against the Spanish Armada in 1587 and again in 1588. This picture shows a sea battle between the Spanish Armada and the English fleet in 1588.

This drum from the 1500s is said to have been owned by Sir Francis Drake. He took this drum with him when he sailed around the world. Later a story was often told about the drum. According to the tale, when England is in danger, Drake's Drum taps a beat. It asks for the help of England's hero, Sir Francis Drake.

Drake Raids the Spanish

In 1585, as relations between England and Spain worsened, Queen Elizabeth **authorized** Sir Francis Drake to sail again to the West Indies. Drake's forces attacked many Spanish towns in the West Indies. However, the people who lived in the towns heard he was coming and ran away with everything valuable. The voyage did not make money, but the English were pleased with Drake's military successes.

Phillip II, king of Spain, began to gather Spanish ships to attack the coast of England. Drake advised the queen to attack before Spain did. On April 2, 1587, an English fleet led by Drake left Plymouth and headed for the Spanish port of Cadiz. Drake planned to stage a raid, or a surprise attack, on the Spanish ships that were gathering there. Drake captured or destroyed between 25 and 39 Spanish ships. He then went on to the Azores, the islands off the coast of Africa, where he captured a Spanish treasure ship.

The Spanish Armada

Sir Francis Drake's raid in Cadiz held back the Spanish attack on England. However, in 1588, Phillip II sent the Spanish **Armada** into the English Channel, the body of water between England and France. The Spanish hoped to gain control of the waterway and **invade** England. Queen Elizabeth prepared the English fleet to defend the channel. Lord Howard of Effington was made England's **naval** commander, and Drake was made his vice **admiral**.

The sea battle began on July 21 near Plymouth. There were many days with no progress. Then the English harmed several Spanish ships on July 29 and forced the rest close to the rocks just past Calais, France. The Spanish ships moved north. A storm then blew the armada farther north. In **defeat** the Spanish sailed north around Scotland. Then it sailed past Ireland in an attempt to reach Spain. Illness and many shipwrecks off the coast of Ireland killed most of the Spanish soldiers and sailors.

Timeline

1540 Francis Drake is born in Tavistock, England.

1562 Drake sails to the West Indies for the first time.

1569 Drake marries Mary Newman.

1572 Drake captures the treasure carried by a Spanish mule train in Central America and returns to England a wealthy man.

1577 Drake begins his voyage around the world.

1579 Drake pauses somewhere on the coast of western North America to fix his ships.

1580 Drake returns to England. He becomes the second man to guide a ship all the way around the world.

1581 Queen Elizabeth knights him, and he becomes Sir Francis Drake.

1583 Drake's wife Mary dies.

1585 He marries Elizabeth Sydenham.

1587 Drake's raid on Cadiz helps hold back the Spanish Armada.

1588 As vice admiral, Drake helps defeat, or beat, the Spanish Armada.

1596 Drake dies on his final voyage and is buried at sea.

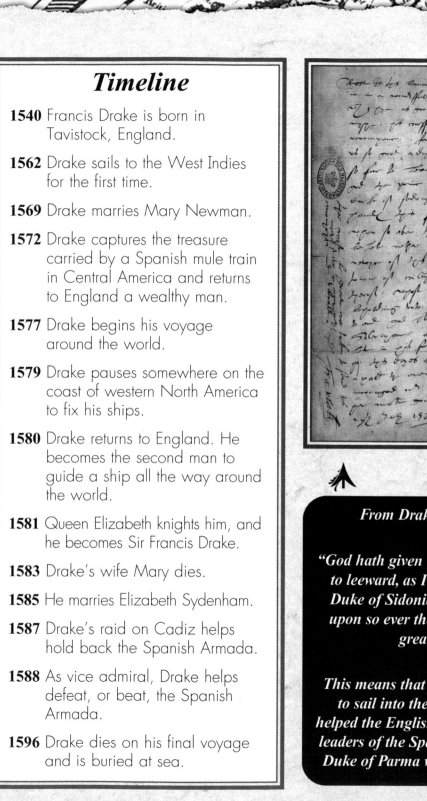

Sir Francis Drake wrote this letter on July 29, 1588, to Sir Frances Walsingham, the queen's secretary. Drake told Walsingham that England had beaten Spain at the Battle of Gravelines.

From Drake's Letter to Sir Francis Walsingham

"God hath given us so good a day in forcing the enemy so far to leeward, as I hope in God the Prince of Parma and the Duke of Sidonia shall not shake hands this few days. And upon so ever they shall meet I believe neither of them will greatly rejoice of this day's service."

This means that because the Spanish ships had been forced to sail into the wind, they were blown off course, which helped the English to win the battle. Drake also joked that the leaders of the Spanish Armada, the Duke of Sedonia and the Duke of Parma would not be happy about losing this battle.

Drake's Last Voyage

In 1595, Drake set off on another voyage to raid the Spanish West Indies. His partner was John Hawkins, the cousin he had sailed with as a young man. The expedition was a failure. The Spanish towns and ships were much better protected than they had been on earlier trips. Sailors on the ships also suffered from a deadly fever. Hawkins became ill and died. Drake got sick, too. On January 28, 1596, he died and was buried at sea.

Before Francis Drake the Spanish and the Portuguese controlled exploration. Drake's success helped turn England into a great naval power. Drake's greatest **achievement**, though, was his trip around the world. Magellan had done it 60 years before Drake, but Magellan's trip was not nearly as successful. Drake kept most of his men alive and healthy, and he kept his ship in good shape. That was a huge accomplishment.

Glossary

achievement (uh-CHEEV-ment) Something great that is done with hard work.

admiral (AD-muh-rul) A naval officer of the highest rank.

amazingly (uh-MAYZ-ing-lee) Wonderfully.

armada (ar-MAH-duh) A large group of warships.

authorized (AH-thuh-ryzd) Gave permission, made legal.

cargoes (KAR-gohz) Loads of goods carried by an airplane, a ship, or an automobile.

defeat (dih-FEET) A loss.

expedition (ek-spuh-DIH-shun) A trip for a special purpose.

fleet (FLEET) Many ships under the command of one person.

invade (in-VAYD) To enter a place to attack and take over.

knighted (NYT-ed) To be made a knight, an honor given by the king or queen for service. Those made knights are able to use the word "Sir" with their names.

mule train (MYOOL TRAYN) A group of mules traveling together in a long, moving line.

mutiny (MYOO-tin-ee) Disobeying a captain's orders.

naval (NAY-vul) Having to do with ships and shipping.

Parliament (PAR-lih-mint) The group in England that makes the country's laws.

pirate (PY-rit) A person who attacks and robs ships.

ports (PORTS) Places on the coast where boats can be tied up and cargo unloaded.

Protestant (PRAH-tes-tunt) Having to do with a Christian belonging to a church that does not look to the pope for guidance.

reef (REEF) Hills of rocks or coral that are near the surface of the water.

strait (STRAYT) A narrow waterway connecting two larger bodies of water.

trade routes (TRAYD ROOTS) Paths used to travel places to buy or sell goods.

treasure (TREH-zher) Things of great worth or value.

valuable (VAL-yoo-bul) Important, or worth lots of money.

voyage (VOY-ij) A journey by water.

Index

Web Sites

Due to the changing nature of Internet links, PowerKids Press has developed an online list of Web sites related to the subject of this book. This site is updated regularly. Please use this link to access the list:

www.powerkidslinks.com/pslfe/drake/

Primary Sources

Cover. Francis Drake. Color engraving. Circa 1585. By W. Holl from an original painting in the possession of Sir T.F. Elliott Drake. **Page 5. Inset.** Sir Francis Drake. Portrait. Circa 1500s. By French artist Isaac Oliver (c. 1565–1617). This is the only known portrait of Drake with red hair. Victoria & Albert Museum, London, Great Britain. **Page 6. Left.** Page from a September 16, 1567, letter to Elizabeth I regarding the triangular trade. Written by Sir John Hawkins. National Archives, Washington, D.C. **Right.** Sir John Hawkins. Watercolor and gouache on paper. Circa 1800s. The portrait, based on a triple portrait by Custodis (done before his death in 1598), appeared in an 1825 publication titled "Memoirs of the Court of Queen Elizabeth." by Sarah, Countess of Essex. **Page 10. Left.** Universal compass. Gold. 1568. By Nikolaus Rensperger. Private Collection, Wuppertal, Germany. **Page 10. Right.** Pirate ship's figurehead. Painted wood. 1600s. Maritiem Museum Prins Hendrik, Rotterdam, Netherlands. **Page 13. Top.** Seal (vitulus marinus). Description and drawing from journal. Journal entry by Chaplain Francis Fletcher, who traveled with Drake on the *Golden Hind*. Drawing was probably done by one of Drake's crew members. British Library, London, Great Britain. **Page 13. Bottom.** South America and the Strait of Magellan. Folio 13 of the Hydrographic Atlas. 1571. By Fernan Vaz Dourado. **Page 14. Top.** *Vera Totius Expeditionis Nauticae*. Hand-colored engraving. Circa 1595. Published by well-known Dutch mapmaker Jodocus Hondius. Map shows the first English expedition around the world by Sir Francis Drake in 1577, and another voyage taken a few years later by Thomas Cavendish in 1586. Margin art includes Elizabethan coat of arms, the *Golden Hind*, and Nova Albion. American Treasures collection of the Library of Congress, Washington, D.C. **Page 17. Bottom.** Tobacco (Petun). Drawing from *Histoire Naturelle des Indes (Natural History of the Indies)*, a translation from the "Drake Manuscript." Circa late 1500s. Pierpont Morgan Library, New York, New York. **Page 18. Top.** Engagement of the English and Spanish Fleets. Engraving. Circa 1739. Depicts sea battle between the English fleet and the Spanish Armada in 1588. Image border contains portraits of admirals, famous people, cherubs, and other designs. British Library, London, Great Britain. **Page 18. Bottom.** Drake's Drum. 1596. Plymouth Art Gallery. Great Britain. **Page 21.** Page from July 29, 1588, letter to Sir Francis Walsingham, Elizabeth I's secretary, after the Battle of Gravelines. Written by Sir Francis Drake. Public Record Office, Topham, Great Britain.